Praise for *How To Hold a Flying River*

Implicit in this irresistible title, *How to Hold a Flying River*, is a poetry of the ineffable and ephemeral, its metaphor striving toward the light and shadow of all we cannot hold: "Shock// of glass. You can't have this moment so why write about nightingales? It//happens when we split ourselves off from ourselves. It has the/right to be difficult." Through irresolvable stories and anecdotes, Martha Kalin captures the crumbling "Tower of Hay" of our lives in memorable and highly-wrought lines:

> —Stop!
> But it can't be stopped,
> not the snow
> of her face or the towel
> of hay as it burns.

- Mark Irwin, author of *American Urn: Selected Poems* (1987-2014)

In *How to Hold a Flying River*, Martha Kalin's poems glisten with thirst, create a shining flow of dreams and desire. We travel luminous meanders of the poet's "memory of water's everywhere," hidden faces and histories hiding in the honest reveal: "Family is an ocean that will swallow you," she tells us. These poems soar with transcendent mystery, the title's glimpse of her impossible paradoxes. Kalin is a poet of unparalleled brilliance.

- Joy Roulier Sawyer, author of *Lifeguards* and *Tongues of Men and Angels*

The haunting beauty of Martha Kalin's poems rest in things seen and not seen, objects and people and emotions resting in the shadows. The poems often ask questions, seeking to know the ways in which we look toward, and then away. These liminal moments happen throughout—and yes, "how terrifying and maddening that radiance," and yes, when I read these poems, I too want to know: "when will it [this radiance] come again"? *How to Hold a Flying River* is a gorgeous, complex book, one I'll be thinking about for a long time.

- Michael Henry, author of *No Stranger Than My Own* and *Active Gods*

Published by
Regal House Publishing, LLC
Raleigh, NC 27612
All rights reserved

ISBN -13 (paperback): 9781646030057
ISBN -13 (epub): 9781646030323
Library of Congress Control Number: 2019941554

Interior and cover design by Lafayette & Greene
lafayetteandgreene.com
Cover images © by TairA/Shutterstock

Regal House Publishing, LLC
https://regalhousepublishing.com

Printed in the United States of America

How to Hold a Flying River

POEMS

Martha Kalin

Regal House Publishing

CONTENTS

Foreword i

Confluence 1

The Hiddenness of Things 2

Autumn 3

What Gathers from Nothing 4

Rearranging the Bones of Your Face 5

Messages from a Concave Dream 6

City 7

Consolation #3, *Lento Placido*, in D-Flat Major 9

Train Ride with Hair on Fire 11

Verbatim: 12

Beautiful Window 13

Tower of Hay 17

Didn't Want to 19

The Truth About Why 20

Listening 21

The Hush a Life Makes 22

Between Your Sleep and Mine 24

Skating Backward 27

A Good Story 29

Beloved 31

Crosswalk 35

Spark 36

Harbors 37

The Singing 38

Sisterhood 40

The Opposite of What Happens 42

Tsunami 43

Shape Shifter 44

Myrtle Along the Steps 45

Brief Feather 47

Nostalgia and Other Rivers. 49

Maps. 53

Where the River Goes. 55

for Sarah 55

Mouths Open for Water 57

Cave of Hands 58

Mojave *(Beside the Water)* *60*

Some Thoughts on Some Trees 61

What Shone. 62

Tchaikovsky's Strings. 63

Consolation #5 in E Major *(Madrigal)* *64*

Refuge 65

No 66

Other Skin. 69

Love Sonnet 70

Inside the Sock Drawer. 71

Lunch at Zaidy's 72

Looking for Your Brother's Grave. 73

Reflection. 74

Migration 75

My Mother Joins the Cloud Appreciation Society. 76

The Sky in the Hole of the Skull .77

Going Outside for the Morning Paper. 78

Out of Time 79

How to Catch Yourself Sleeping .80

Undressed 81

How to Hold a Flying River 82

Notes 85

Acknowledgements. 87

Foreword

Zack Rogow

How to Hold a Flying River is different from any other writing I've ever read. Martha Kalin hits so many different notes in her writing: vulnerable, wounded, celebratory, powerful, lyrical, tender, and prophetic. The tone can range from earthy to exquisite, often in the same poem. She reports accurately and bravely on the pains of aging, violence, and defeat, but even in the most trying situations, she shows that the soothing qualities of beauty are always within reach. She displays the strength of the heart and of human connection with a visionary splendor. This is a world where purity and sophistication can exist side by side.

Kalin often visits nature in her poems, and she finds so much there. She explores both the puzzles of darkness and the healing of luminosity. Kalin has the ability to continually surprise us, whisking us from everyday moments to memorable depths:

This is the restless hour, when a woman, searching, might look up through a hole in the clouds

might taste that butter the bees know, drink the silver of last night's rain clinging to webs stretched

blade to blade

"Consolation #5 in E Major *(Madrigal)*"

It was my pleasure to select her as the winning recipient of Regal House Publishing's 2019 Terry J. Cox Poetry Award.

for Locksley

Is not impermanence the very fragrance of our days?

- Rainer Maria Rilke

CONFLUENCE

A line of moons, swans out of water, a family posed
at the scenic overlook. On fire, sulky. The father's lips form
a circle, his head tilted up, singing. Inside are invisible things.

Family is an ocean that will swallow you. The last time driving
together through West Virginia, scent of road dust and Alzheimer's,
my father spoke of his regrets and the dark waters parted.

Eau de vie, water of life, aged in oak barrels 3 to 100 years. Aromas
vary with age: vanilla, nuts, flowers, slight swirl, come closer, inhale.
Trebbiano. Delicate, well-rounded. Born of chalky soil and ocean.

Meanwhile, there's this:

THE HIDDENNESS OF THINGS

As a child I thought I could hide like a door inside a closet,
far away and close at the same time—could oppose everything
    and everything would stop.

Sometimes at night, behind the veil of crickets and clockwork
of trains, I'd see a globe spinning inside my head, hear high notes
    arc and arc until finally I'd sleep.

I look angry in the picture my father took at an overlook
    on the way to visit my grandparents.

Eight hours winding through coal towns, discontent
    simmering, a crack in the windshield.

My sister kept throwing up in weeds by the roadside,
my mother turned her head away
    every time we veered around a curve.

What is it that makes us care about someone?

In junior high I wrote a story about being buried alive
    and the teacher wouldn't look at me.

When my grandmother began not making sense,
her fingers would flitter, blue veins
    traveling her hands, arms, disappearing

in distant sleeves—

AUTUMN

The day turned soft and slow, shorter
      than in summer, and they stopped what they were doing

when her father came home from the plant. A foursome,
      they pulled aluminum folding chairs
            onto the patio, easing into crickets, a single rope
                swinging from the limb of a mulberry.

She stood in a leaf pile, watched him lighten
      with each sweep of the rake. Humming,
            flannel shirt flapping open. *Please
              give me a word for this:*

the heat of an explosion, molten metal
      from the chemical factory shredding
            the dusky sky. A firefly, flying erratically,
                uneasy with its release from inside a jar.

WHAT GATHERS FROM NOTHING

Some treasures aren't found, but circle outside time
dark and numinous, the way storm clouds gather from nothing
and notes from a blues song slink upstairs when I'm trying to sleep

The sky is crying—Elmore James and the Broomdusters

Flash   hesitant slip of   wait
wait   rolling growling gnashing   bite

I climb out and off the brutal blue roof into the muted

afterward—leaving a trail of buttons and string
down the canyon road split open by flood, light bending, bowing
shimmering through bits of leftover flesh

Rearranging the Bones of Your Face

What do you want you ask as if I were a cloud-swallowed moon
which means I may or may not be visible. My mind flings answers,
rearranging the bones of your face. The heart is a muscle and
the sudden desire to run is like being shot in the back.

I've been such an idiot for not yelling I hate you across the
brooding kitchen, spooling back love under cloud cover, why can't
you see it.

How wide is that river, are both banks the same?

The refrigerator that Paul Reps says is the source of our suffering
keeps humming—go ahead annoy me refrigerator with your
humming even in the midst of sex I've changed since that first
New Years when we uncorked champagne, smashing the kitchen
window into a question mark.

Messages from a Concave Dream

When I say something not fully formed what follows is loneliness.
I get up to make coffee and find little messages in my spoon: today
today today. Dream-walking

I hand the baby over to a rickety bus ferrying up
the mountain—who is this woman handing over her baby? Trust?
Fear? I hand the baby over, the window a black hole in a state of

intense unrest, I get in alongside, the wound a womb the soul
returns to for safekeeping—

what I want to say but can't say to the baby-faced,
wound-up-with-love young man beside me: it's not as easy
as you say, there's a knife edge that can cut off your tongue—
a strange mutant joy in trying to understand one another—

how little our time, how wild my love, how terrifying
and maddening that
radiance, when will it come again.

CITY

A city is a kind of memory
—Jake Adam York

Welcome, you might say—if the door were open, if you were
that kind of city. If it weren't too much to carry.

A woman rushes by chattering to another. *I'm worried*—she says,
worried—sapphire dress rushing by, shiny-black shoes rushing by.

Vet's sign: *homeless humiliated sorry*

At 19 I came to you, city where I didn't belong.
A job at Amalgamated Life Insurance, short-short flowered dress,
walk down Broadway to Union Square, catcalls, morning sleeper
tucked inside a garbage can.

The only non-Jew of the group of ladies, they taught me to turn
the giant card machine at perfect speed, read inscrutable signatures,
make kugel. My job: to check index cards for duplicates,
names of the dead, $3 an hour.

You can't abandon your history, and it won't abandon you

I return to you, the way one does. The 4th floor walk-up
where we lived, glossy black door, begonias on the stoop, Saturday,
late afternoon. How does one unlodge it? Why I felt violated
walking to work, exposed, unable

to return.

Did we love each other in that single bed? White cat calling
from the small brick courtyard below: an air of

sadness for all the city can't surface. How am I connected

how am I
connected? Who said *let's move* who said *you're sapping me I can't*

learn to love the brittle open blind
improvise
let in whatever
wants to
come

Consolation #3, *Lento Placido*, in D-Flat Major

after Franz Liszt

I go back and forth on retirement. Yes, there will be time
for walking when the air's still cool. No, I won't use my time well.

When the shower curtain billows as if someone entered the house
and a homeless man asks me for fifty cents I say no. But when my
wallet's stolen by some maestro of lost identity along with dental
floss and the keys to my house the yes/no balance begins to shift—

      it's time to go.

I leave for Florida the next day to see my mom. We walk
on the beach in blustery winds looking for shells.

Most things I worry about come to nothing and the future
surprises me. Now, coming out the other side of the worry tunnel,
I remember the outline of my grandparents' home
on Linden Street—

      a form

of consolation. Clouds float by as if on piano keys, as if morning
would always love evening, silhouettes changed by what the other
is. I come back to our feet in sand, the buoyancy of the kite surfer,
our passage into a certain/uncertain

      future—

present as I sit with my mother on the boardwalk looking at silver memorial plaques of family members who once watched the sunset too. *Will you make one for me?* It wakes my eye, a bubble of air inside water, iridescent scalloping of a shell.

TRAIN RIDE WITH HAIR ON FIRE

My name is Haley says the stylist, as she swivels my chair.
Tells me of her

train ride from Kansas— so many cows in Eastern Colorado!
I see

a goddess emblazoned on her arm, swirls
of indigo and vermillion from shoulder to wrist.

She texturizes, feathers, sprays me with bergamot, rubs
my forehead with the tip of a thumb. Glows as she tilts

my head back. Oh eater of stars, how far can one bend?
The mist keeps me from igniting though my hair's

(must one push against reality to find it?)

burning: I don't know how to stop it.

Verbatim:

To enter worlds different than the ordinary, lie down for a while.
Let some weary possibility that refuses to speak, speak. Shock
of glass.

You can't have this moment so why write about nightingales? It
happens when we split ourselves off from ourselves. It has the
right to be difficult.

To wander you have to go on wandering. When I'm gone what will
my feet look like? Small pools, needles of fir, vast whipped clouds,
bits of linen.

You are missing—he's missing. She's happier in the country with
only time. A vanishingly small chance to find something there
between the stars.

They are bold brilliant beautiful. Incubators. Bawling, grabbing,
holding, hugging. Together creating together.

A spell is a transfer from one to another, harvest of sand in the
crease of the neck. To close your eyes believing the moon is still
there. To drift.

Blue door, blue lake, collective nakedness. What the universe needs.
Moths stirring along old stone steps ring the riverine path.

Beautiful Window

in the inner chamber of the eye it's deep and quiet

    in it the iris is round and reactive

any surface glistening undulating

    has that kind of beauty   water remaking

        the contours of land

evening-textured air   wax sliding down

    the side of a candle   glint of a buckle   gold circling

       a wrist   smoke of a hum

oh my daughter we're born of many things

    violets violations violence   #movementsmatter

       matter   matter

into the dream where Alice went:

    if someone says *don't be afraid* do you believe it?

dilemmas unfold   the flutter

        of wings in our ears   miniature

                boats whisked out to sea

I am that/not that

        red flounder sunset   oyster shell   minnows

past the eye a beautiful window:

        absolutely still   irresolvable depth and lights left on

TOWER OF HAY

Decades later
it still waits
for understanding

to rise from the gritty
field of sleep—
locks me in

my own raw throat.
Five years old, I'm
with my family, traveling

through open
country when
a barn's struck

by a fork
of lightning—and
the summer night

lets loose.
The car that once
held us safe from

the whirring dark
grows icy, I
shatter, a body

splintered, a million
pieces that won't
be stilled.

My father's hands
on the wheel
are helpless as daisies.

Mama half turns,
grips the seat—*Stop!*
But it can't be stopped,

not the snow
of her face or the tower
of hay as it burns.

DIDN'T WANT TO

Practice. Raged against scales, black painted wood and ivory keys.
Raged against my mother who still raged against her mother—
all the way to those cold ivory teeth. Didn't want to take a bath
so I raged. Raged into the heat, into the tiles, into the washcloth I
tried to cover myself with when my father came in to ask
why I was so mad at my mother. How could he understand?
I wrote poems, stuffed them into a little door inside the bathroom
closet for some future me who'd understand when her daughter
slams the door so hard it makes all the paintings in the house jump.

THE TRUTH ABOUT WHY

Why I always left the door open a crack, had to hear the moans of parents making love, why the skinny cat was free to come and go, why my mother's words struck me, a cold wind on my neck, why I didn't cry when the man in the woods put his hands down my pants across from the lumber yard on a Saturday morning, why I ran and ran to tell my parents, why they never spoke of it or held me close because of it, why hunger's flare drives out air, why anger is glass broken into fine enough pieces to walk on, why I stop sleeping in any familiar way, why thoughts are wolves that stalk my silence, why they won't be stilled for anyone.

LISTENING

Had you been here
between then and now
you would have heard

what my other self hears,

the one that nests
on the top of my head:
listening, listening.

I wish I knew
what comes next.
I know it's not spring

or walks without purpose.

Is each weed a soldier?
Is the earth not tender?
Which part of my silence

did I not want you to hear?

THE HUSH A LIFE MAKES

Maybe in spring
I'll take the winding
road out west,

climb the shoulder
of Lookout Mountain,
find overhead

what pierces, or down
below the hush a life
makes walking a stream

at dusk: jagged ice islands,
snow boulders dissolving
in the newly mild air—

but for now I'll
head east toward
the familiar

slice of moon—I'll
remember and forget
and remember again

how but not why
you turned and fled
down the stairs with your

bag and didn't stumble
or acknowledge that
you wanted this

to end—blue
nylon, it held
just a few things:

a pair of jeans, a sweater—
when you grabbed it from
the floor and left

what you clutched was
a rope you dragged
all the way across town

to the peeling brown
house with its sad
windows—the house

I said I could never
live in, a rope that wove—
as we unwove—up the stairs

and onto the bed,
your light caress,
endless thank-you's.

BETWEEN YOUR SLEEP AND MINE

> *Hark ye yet again, the little lower layer...If man must*
> *strike, strike through the mask! How can the prisoner*
> *reach outside except by thrusting through the wall?*
> —Herman Melville

Six years after your cancer
you live in a different time:

the thud of apples as they drop
on the roof in the night

signals a shift,
a gathering of seeds,

each singly pressed
burst of tree released

down the shingled slope
to land at your door.

Light lasts longer, bronzes
fields where roots

once sheltered slave blood.
The past is just a skin

you don't hold on to.
A beautiful woman

rescues your severed fingers
and puts them on ice.

❧

Slow melting summer
making love on 100 count threads

of spun cotton.
Come in I say, and in your dream

a blonde woman walks
right through the wall into the room.

❧

Rows of cotton
pickers move in rounded waves.

You learned your
lesson—never

let anyone see you give a white
girl a gift.

❧

You give me flowers, first a peony
picked from the shade of the apple tree,

barely open, pale, but then
it starts to bloom and just goes

on, a blonde who
makes herself at home.

Get out of here! you scream, and I'm
not certain who you're talking to.

Then one red rose in a slender vase,
then three, then eighteen tiny buds.

&

Everything I have is steeped
in privilege—

waking early and returning
to sleep

as if there will always be more.
The cooing dove on my balcony

reminds me of Melville's
little lower layer—the white wall

that helps me sleep keeps you,
your reassembled black fingers awake.

SKATING BACKWARD

I should have known
where we were headed

but lose my
concentration

watching skaters
on the rink,

revolutions of lean-
legged teens,

bright jackets
flapping open, lit

glass globes
strung from pines.

Legs, once trustworthy,
go awry,

eyes and toes
get slammed into

a quivering
retreat as the last

clouds slide east,
past the crackle

of the speakers
and the anthem

singer's futile
words—oh yes

we could have
loved each other better.

A Good Story

It starts to unravel halfway through—
or maybe sooner—though it's a good
story—I'm more interested

in how the rain puddles,
submerging neon lights into
reflective lines of Saturday night

and people going places. Soon
his story's putting me to sleep, or is it
the warm tortillas.

I know exactly where he's going,
even if I don't know how,
can see the well-worn

neurons firing, can
picture all the others who
have heard this story too.

I try to interrupt but he won't
be stopped, a runaway train
and I'm tied to the tracks.

I don't believe he notices
the steaming windows, that our
elbows touch, or the hypnotic

sliver of confetti twisting
over the bar. My senses
blur, begin to pull him

from the shadows—no longer
a table between us, I hear
flute notes climbing a vast

wall of space, his knee
nudging mine, a sensation impossible
to translate, it has no meaning

in and of itself, stories are
stitched together like stars that only
pulse when another star is near.

BELOVED

Next time I fall in love
I'll think of her
in her multi-colored muumuu,

large-hipped, not even
a little embarrassed when
I introduce the man

I hope won't be embarrassed
by her. Me? A little strange.
Weird my friends said.

I wasn't at ease with
myself or chatter,
wrote dark poems,

longed for sex
more than friendship,
wanted it to feel the way

poems made me feel—all
that can happen
will happen, ecstasy

will build on ecstasy,
meaning can be
found even if

I must find it
over and over.
Is this the beloved

prophets sing of?
I dream I'm riding
my bike so fast

downhill that I
sail over the abyss
to land in

a room of
strangers—we stand
breast to breast,

hair electric,
arms outspread—
my great wild mother.

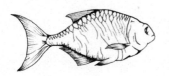

CROSSWALK

A slow walker along the graveled margins of the road, bright-
bearded, untoothed, reaching out

bucket-handed for the next generation to rise with its impatiences,
redyellowgreen—hell—you lose

the right to cross, forget the ones who walk about confused as
leaves, tin-footed, fruit-skinned—

and look how uncontained the clouds that fill him,
fumble-eyed, he veers

then plants himself, a burned pole, he'll stay until light's concrete
and Earth itself flattened.

SPARK

Before the road begins its rise
through Commerce City,
smokestacks smudge the mountains
yellow and gray, an arm
draped flag-like
from the barrel of a truck flicks
a cigarette out the window, it flitters into dry weeds along the gully
—and I
                    look back and
back across the indifferent plains retreating
in the haze, search the sky for
elegance, order
the fluid arrow of geese
heading south, anything but
the word *again* plastered to my neighbor's bumper, what comes after
make, after *America*, after *great*.

HARBORS

She startles at the least
bit of mystery, my coworker,
so we celebrate the day with cake
in the break room, red corn syrup
flowers, the vigilance
it takes to fend off a dead father's
abuses, oceanic
pressure, crushing tides—the key
to visual appeal is sharp
petaled red against white—flight from
sheer to deep to light to—harbors
gone dark—and lost are
thin filaments that would allow her to breathe.

THE SINGING

pool her father built with coins that jingled
in his pockets, when he came singing
home, tender
        of the bar, pool that drowned

the dog—built it for the bride
he took from her adobe
village weaving sandals out of straw—
                          to show how much he
loved the son,
son who filled the pool with dirt, turned it to a garden,
left his mother with that dying

bed, snuck into his sister's lifelong—

view broken now
with weeds, not
             sure about

the pool, especially the pool, hates
the garden, tends the garden so her mother will have flowers,
mother's eyes are turned away—
                 falls into
the hay and welts erupt, her
hands breed thorns, she picks them out,
hands exploding

into pain, smoothes them with a
tincture, soothes the way her father
                      would, instead

he screams, her mother goes downstairs to sew
pockets on his trousers, wants to
feel her body there beside him,

                                 who knows
that pool, its singing

SISTERHOOD

I had not asked for such a blood sisterhood
—Sylvia Plath

I eat it by accident, a large
blackberry, hiding in a clump of grapes
under the spinach leaves.

Pushing up his sleeves, a man reveals
the beginnings of skin, muscle and bone.
No other women at the table, I feel

alone. Come closer, I want
to look at you *that way.* Power
lines undulating through low clouds.

❧

Near Alamosa hundreds of semi's
loading potatoes.
Further north, in the Iron Horse room,

old photos of trains with historic names: *Mogul,
Consolidation, Car Forward.*
I come across her poem *Blackberrying*

❧

as I lie in the grass at a summer festival.
Balloons swirl into the apex
of the band-shell, flies, the smell of grilled meat.

I didn't ask for this kind of sisterhood.
I find her tied up in the garage with blood on her knees.
I find her with her head in the oven.

When I turn she's gone. The din
of a silversmith beating on intractable metal.
The only thing to come now is the sea.

THE OPPOSITE OF WHAT HAPPENS

Her voice rattles the tables
of the Blue Lagoon, first left off Peoria.

Some days the world breaks you
through no fault of its own.

We're held together, two pairs
of eyes and a blood

moon eclipse—but that's not how
the world will end. I try

to do what's expected and she does
the opposite. Puts pain pills and cigarettes in

jewel cases, hides them under leaves
with names like *where nothing blooms.*

Outside it clouds, almost rains,
demon of a bus almost runs over me. It's Peoria.

I wait to hear her story, the way
a sister would. *So tired, I'm tired*

she tells me, nothing
about jewel cases, the hidden, the room

that wants answers but can't find them, voids
filling the walls with those pictures of Brazilian orchids.

Tsunami

What do they want, these dream-men, who hold us
hostage in the still point of night, in the vast elusive dark
sinking sand, who salt-spray

our mouths open, after hiding the key, before
the deluge, before almost everything goes
under, the massive growing wall and its endless curl—

❧

My feet glow red as they thrust themselves out from blankets
even on the coldest night, the tumbling disarray of
thoughts, too many pillows, are they mine? I think I hear silence

breathing, faster than light, pounding from the left side of my chest,
and there it is, what I do not want to frighten away from, the key
placed carefully on a shelf.

❧

In the San Francisco airport gates open like savage
eaters of all that's solid. So many hours to kill.

Let the hours and their expectations go. In the dream the women
are small, disfigured, colorful, and real and I am

one of them. And the bent-over crone who presses her finger like a
key to my forehead, devouring, filling, she is one of us.

SHAPE SHIFTER

Just try to shape yourself into something
like clouds

unfurling in the sky's
blue wind. You can't.

When your ass is pinched on buses
you simply split apart,

when your boss slides a fevered
hand down your pants

you don't feather or coil, you don't become anything except
residue.

What is there to say about
fog?

Lives shatter
just trying to get to the border.

I tell you go spend a day in the pain
clinic,

oh mountain waiting to soften, go ask for help, go
ask for help.

MYRTLE ALONG THE STEPS

The patient's legs and arms are
carved with scars,

etched with tries
she's made to die.

She curls into my own
wounds on the exam table,

eyes filled with mud.
Please let me out.

❧
Blue glass bottles in every
window, every window
thick, leaded.

My friend wonders how
I deal with the larger issues:
inequity, injustice.

There are infinities I want
to feel, but not always
the one in front of me.

❧
The myrtle along the steps
has shiny leaves and white star-like
flowers—the patient dies

45

over and over. What if
we could see the maze from a great
distance, darkness mingling

easily with
light, see the way out
as we go in, is this too much? To inhale

pain as if it were the ever-
lingering fragrance of a dark-
berried shrub.

BRIEF FEATHER

For one brief feather
of a moment she's not

in the waiting room
at the end of her life

but an owl
tucked and ready.

A baby coos.
A pregnant woman turns

her head down.
Many of all types

wait to be called,
but it's she whose

flight sweeps
fear from its spool,

the leading edges
of her wings

serrated
like the teeth of a comb.

She doesn't look back
through the swinging

door marked exit, glides
to the furthest limb

of the furthest pine,
her talons

gilded with
the sharpness of swords.

Nostalgia and Other Rivers

When we fall in love again
     with the river, we'll look back on
          its flooded banks—our small

blue tent will have
     paddles and clouds
          of swallows will fill the sky.

We'll look back on the current
     whose surge severs
          trees from roots, tongues

from mouths, and, as Great
     Grandma Anna instructed us
          we'll carry our containers

of chicken soup carefully
     home on the subway.
          We'll be good to one another.

MAPS

How easy it is to be enslaved
      by a castle or a rhythm,

      a thought or a thistle, twitched
by wind, lost in sage, stung by the wizardry of stars

as if those flecks of distant rocks could break us
      into love.

      Did someone once
hold me by the shoulders, tilt my head up, trace

the dipper on the side of my neck until silence knew
      all the regions where light begins?

The map I'm looking for is the endless
      unfolding kind they don't make anymore—

      long cold car trip around the Great Lakes
all the way to Montreal, forty below, gas lamps

in the French quarter, selves so far from themselves
      I find again what I've always found—

Don't worry, I tell the man who keeps showing up,
      a bellman at my door, *you're a fantasy, easy to let go of.*

      He tells me he longs to see me
in a silk nightgown the moment after waking.

My mother never gives me advice
　　　but the psychic in a house full of crosses does

　　　as she surveys my tea leaves and maps
my palm: *beware of a man who knows all the right words to say.*

I get what she sees in the bitter
　　　leaves—so easy to be held captive

　　　or jostled into place
by routes that lead—where do they lead?

A patch of light spills across the living
　　　room floor and a red lacquer dragon

　　　leaps resplendent
off the smooth white mantle.

WHERE THE RIVER GOES

for Sarah

Years ago when my daughter
loved nothing better
than Winnie the Pooh,

Saturdays were days
to fill ourselves with
a story read over

and over under layers
of blankets piled on
wide wooden floors.

We'd pry ourselves out
from turning pages
and go to the Nature Center,

spring across plank
bridges to play
the floating stick game.

We'd tip our heads
over the railing,
laughing as our sticks—

so unlike swans—would
tumble, twirl or hit a logjam
caught in leaves—

two ponds, four bridges—
a story that didn't tell us
where the river goes.

MOUTHS OPEN FOR WATER

for Theo

At first the boy's feet are hurting, the rusty
pump's not working, he doesn't love
the jacaranda and fuzzy pink bottle blossoms
that sprinkle the schoolyard like upturned
bells—mouths open for water.
He doesn't yet know

how lush the morning turns
when bougainvillea petals slide under doors,
but soon enough shrieks at the flurry
of mallards, clamber of turtles
from the mud pond, the opening and closing of
an old green chest with a raspy clasp.

CAVE OF HANDS

Pinturas Canyon, Argentina

Like the blind
signals of bats

echoing against
naked cliffs,

these rust
red silhouettes

of palms,
fingers fanned,

must mean
to tell us something—

maybe hearts are like this
when they flit

into the dark of
woods, hover over

rock outcroppings,
find homes

in crevices
among the scraggy

brush, cling
to rough dust-

covered sandstone—
to feel, and feel again.

MOJAVE (BESIDE THE WATER)

Desert tortoises rest in rectangles of shade

    under the solar panels—

        in the grinding nothingness of sand, snags

    of prickly pear, mesquite, creosote—

a Joshua Tree stands like an old Paiute

    with arms raised over the dried-up Pipe Spring—

        the memory of water's everywhere

    on the drained edges of basin and range, one world

pressed into another, in steep cracks or cradles.

Just after sunset the sky breaks into a firestorm

    of stars, not all at once—and strangely

        not so distant now—we drink from

    the shattered night, a bed of crushed shells underneath.

SOME THOUGHTS ON SOME TREES

Some are geometric and angry

Some diminished as birds with limp wings

Some stand in the distance with the vagueness of fathers

Some we'll never know their stories

Some make strange whistling sounds in their sleep

Some have been in these woods so long they will always be lost

Some creak and moan for this

For some the lost thing is sky

Some will never die in the teeth of a stranger

Some wear anxieties like leaves

Some throw fruit in the mouth of hunger

Some have voids where they let the wind in

Some become whatever dresses are made of

Some hunch into their own yellowing

Some are ladders that harden into bones

Some lie down in memory of a body, some

give shade from the puzzling light

What Shone

From far around the generous curve

a turtle's head stretches out

from its shell, haloed with light, little shoes

running under backyard oaks, crunch of dead leaves—

brooding witness of hens—

while deep in forests, where wars are small

and chaos endless, many women

have left emblems behind

as I let one fall from my balcony

in a dark-scented dream.

TCHAIKOVSKY'S STRINGS

Night scatters stars like windswept

petals, and moonlight

can't explain the madness of willows stirring up dust, this way,

that—patternless worries blown

against doors—the pavement's glow

uncloaks the snarl of other voices,

what Tchaikovsky knew about strings—

the leaves come down in one big sigh.

CONSOLATION #5 IN E MAJOR (MADRIGAL)

after Franz Liszt

A bee circles the charred stump, catches a smoke-scented wave,
dives into the bush with its buttery blossoms,

circles again.

From the wrangle of scrub a crow squawk overwhelms the trill
of an unfamiliar songbird—warbler, meadowlark, scarlet tanager?

This is the restless hour, when a woman, searching, might look up
through a hole in the clouds

might taste that butter the bees know, drink the silver of last night's
rain clinging to webs stretched

blade to blade, might
share something of life: an accumulation of whirred bee songs.

REFUGE

Unwinding of fleece, time

to feel the vibrant, fleeting

world, large carved god ears that listen

like ponds under sunrise, red streaks

on a stone forehead, sky knocking treetops, frogs

with night-stories, echoes of another beauty—

coming, coming, just beyond.

On the sill a blotch of stain

marks the grinding, sticking window—

breath releases, grief

squeezed from a slow moving dream,

one, two, three, four—

loves thrum from the forest of memory,

a temple of sticks inscribed in fog.

No

When I couldn't go back I drove until I was lost—

when the doors flew open on the side of the mountain

what did I imagine would be let out? The bright

flag of solitude's retreat has been cut

and sewn into a quilt—something emerges

from the parting of lips, too tender for words.

OTHER SKIN

Show me how
to love you, hidden
in some other skin,

hope clinging
like a shirt
I want you to unbutton,

the acres, walls,
uncertain worlds
between us—know that

you're the one
who gives my heart its range,
my feet their grass—

calls out to me, but
I can't hear
what others hear,

really, not now, maybe
never will I learn
how I love to feel

the other side, its
shadows and its shade,
how will I know,

my knowing often
wrong—you, so often
flickering.

LOVE SONNET

Sundays when it rains
we go to the library, down
the center aisle, past
the section on gardening in pots.

We set ourselves loose
in the earth of Neruda's
17th sonnet.
The smell of salt rose,

like dark arrows
from a fire, burrows
so deep in our bodies
we love because we must.

INSIDE THE SOCK DRAWER

When the night's thousand eyes stop you

from sleeping, there's pleasure in the damp

dawn's turn to contemplation of death, oh

I believe I'll live on in some form you tell me,

peering in on tangles of blue and black.

LUNCH AT ZAIDY'S

for Dan, 1952-2012

You'd studied it
for years, knew

so much of dying—
how hungry
sunlight devours

you—shadows,
bones and all.

The waitress whisks
away your plate
as if you are not there.

We speak of magic
but know nothing of magic,

only the bold
brightening of leaves
before they loosen their

hold. Last glimpse: you
blazing down First Street,

a container with half
a club sandwich, nothing in this
world left to know.

Looking for Your Brother's Grave

for Wil

You without
I—

you
looking for
him—

alternating
names—

little blowing
flags of
grass.

REFLECTION

Walk with me there,
where the unrippled

pond becomes itself
riveting: where reeds

silken in eddies,
where the smallest seed's

pried free from
spires of juniper,

where shafts of light
roil rapids

and pines simply meld
into long blue shade.

We walk on, we hold on,
each moving each,

the bush, the brook,
the glistening.

MIGRATION

Above the river's curve the sky
billows—the flapping sounds

familiar like the opening lines of Madame Bovary:
The cap was new. Its peak shone.

Moments of grace break beyond anything known, movements
of light spark rustling overhead, a cloud

of raucous cranes drops from breathlessness
to breath.

MY MOTHER JOINS THE CLOUD APPRECIATION SOCIETY

Piece by piece she grows
    age lines, plays tug of war with gravity.

As blue gray eyes begin to fade,
    she waits to see what might come of clouds.

Cirrus, stratus, cumulus, nimbus.
    Curl, layer, mass, rain.

In the absence of knowing she trusts
    the poet's lines, *sleeping is not death.*

Crossing the stream, she bows
    over the filament that was the bridge's railing—

a curious image in the moving water:
    how much of God does a cloud weigh?

The Sky in the Hole of the Skull

after Georgia O'Keefe

It takes time to see, but there it is, a small river

      creasing through mounds of clay

into a pond where an exchange takes place—

      white space for black line—

one prayer for another. Blue always, and a portal—

      a hole in the universe.

Dagger of sunset becomes a fuzzy

      glow— geometry of mountains, the outline of a skull.

Lines that might be love float seaward.

      Outside the plane window the canvas explodes

with all the flowers from the back of my heart.

GOING OUTSIDE FOR THE MORNING PAPER

A canvas of winter, the frost orange
and gold. Soon we'll
come out to walk our dogs, stepping carefully

around iced corners.
Before the sun rising in the bitter air
turns slant roofs blue.

If I touch it will it go away? In a world where
tiny one of a kind snowflakes on the windshield only last
long enough to nudge the edges of the others they land with

is it important why
we long for tenderness? Even the gray after
the blaze holds

the dimming lamplight of morning—
alone together or stretching out our different hands.
I'd like to hold one now, before day fills in.

OUT OF TIME

From the roughs of throats

  ah's flare like bright

ladies in feathered hats—

  if there's no time then time's

notion melts into glass

  leaving thoughts mopping the corridor.

Inside the friendship room

  a large picture window

faces the sloping lily garden—

  we admire spirals

and the iridescent

  hummingbird's frenzy,

love when wheels hiss

  in front of domed buildings,

sparks bedevil clocks,

  who knows what roundness means?

How to Catch Yourself Sleeping

Turn your
thirst inward

become round as
an empty bowl

invite the leaving
of polished stones

sway like an owl
on the ends of bamboo

dream of yourself
as an intruder

recreate all
you can't remember

vanish in the net
of your tongue's seeking

Undressed

Another form of

      sleep turns over,

the very tip

      of a wave.

I begin to believe

      the universe

delivers us—

      tumble-shelled, comet-dusted—

then dissipates

      into the last slip

of ocean,

      leaving the skin's

sharp fragrance,

      and little air

between us.

How to Hold a Flying River

We keep forgetting
      the receding of hairlines,

      we do this together—

unknowable owls

feather branches,
      leftover leaf-light

penetrates
      the dense valley floor.

Beds springing from walls stir juices
      so old we keep forgetting

the room has no ceiling—oh heaven

      rest your head on my knees—

this is how to hold a flying river.

NOTES

The book's epigraph is from Rainer Maria Rilke's poem "Wild Love" translated by Joanna Macy.

"Confluence" borrows and alters language from a *New York Times* interview with cognac master blender Renaud Fillioux de Gironde: "Cognac Demands Patience and an Educated Nose."

"Rearranging the Bones of Your Face" refers to American artist and poet Paul Reps, author of *Zen Flesh, Zen Bones*.

"City" borrows from Jake Adam York's poem "City of Grace."

"Consolation #3, Lento Placido in D-Flat Major" and "Consolation #5 in E Major (Madrigal)" borrow their titles and inspiration from the Consolations, a series of six solo piano works by Franz Liszt.

"Between Your Sleep and Mine" borrows from Herman Melville's *Moby Dick*.

"Sisterhood" borrows from Sylvia Plath's poem "Blackberrying."

"Some Thoughts on Some Trees" references John Ashbery's poem "Some Trees."

"No" references Jean Valentine's poem "Door in the Mountain."

"Love Sonnet" references Pablo Neruda's Sonnet #17 from *100 Love Sonnets*, translated by Mark Eisner.

"Inside the Sock Drawer" references the jazz classic "The Night Has a Thousand Eyes", music by Jerry Brainin, lyrics by Buddy Bernier.

"Migration" borrows from *Madame Bovary* by Gustave Flaubert.

"My Mother Joins the Cloud Appreciation Society" borrows from W. B. Yeats' poem "At Galway Races."

"The Sky in the Hole of the Skull" was inspired by various Georgia O'Keefe paintings displayed at the Georgia O'Keefe Museum in Santa Fe, New Mexico.

Acknowledgements

I'd like to thank the following journals and websites where these poems, or earlier versions, were first published:

Anastamos: "Tsunami"
Inklette: "Cave of Hands"
Hospital Drive: "Myrtle Along the Steps"; "Brief Feather"
Panoply: "Train Ride with Hair on Fire"
San Pedro River Review: "Mojave (Beside the Water)"

My deepest appreciation also to Chris Ransick and the Poetry Book Project at Lighthouse Writers Workshop where this book was conceived.